Approved by LEO

The finest seal of approval based on taste, looks and durability. All done by my son Leo at 1,5 years old.

Publisher: Skyborn Works
Ilustrations: Simon Zingerman
Typography: Block Pro+, Knewave, FF Providence Sans and Interstate.
OFL: The font software Knewave is licensed under the SIL Open Font License, Version 1.1. Author: Tyler Finck, Copyright © 2010.

ISBN

ISBN-13: 978-91-980904-4-4

CONTACT INFO

Skyborn Works, Lyckselevagen 38, LGH 1102. 162 67 Vallingby. SWEDEN.
T: +46 73 649 83 11
contact@skybornworks.com

www.futurelittle.com
www.skybornworks.com

STOVE

APRON

ROLLING PIN

MIXING BOWLS

MEASURING CUPS

TIMER

DECORATING TOOLS

STAND
MIXER

INGREDIENTS

DOUGH

CAKE

FUDGE

CUPCAKES

COOKIE

PIE

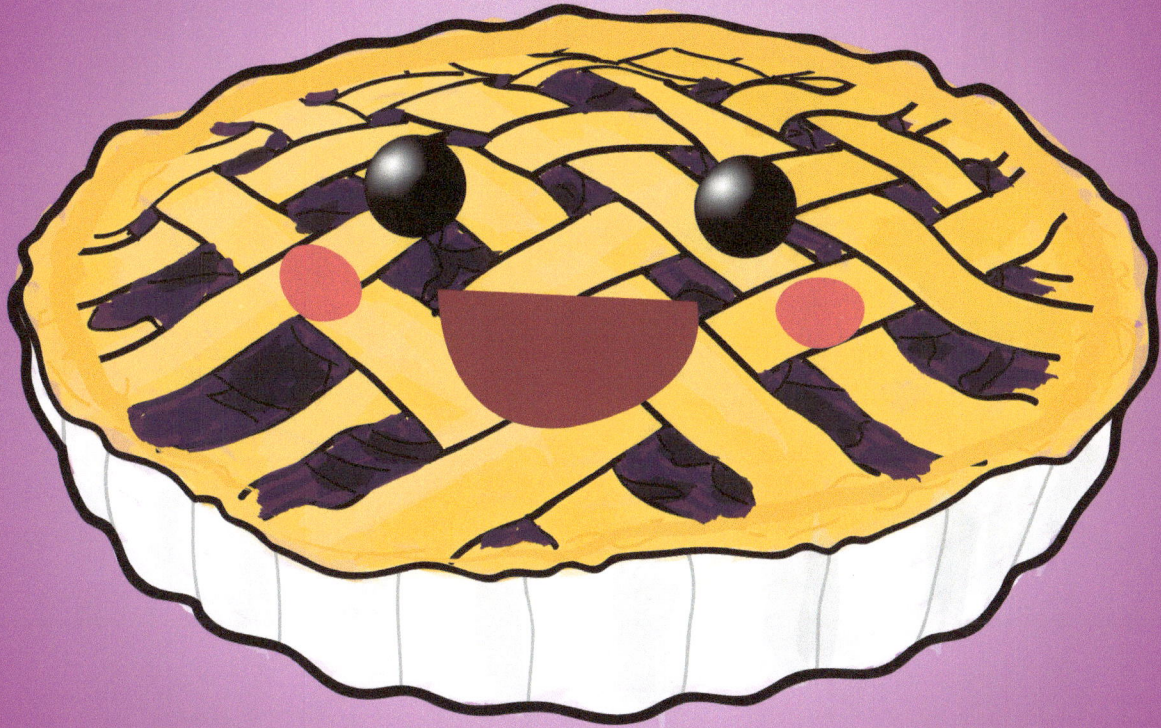

BROWNIE

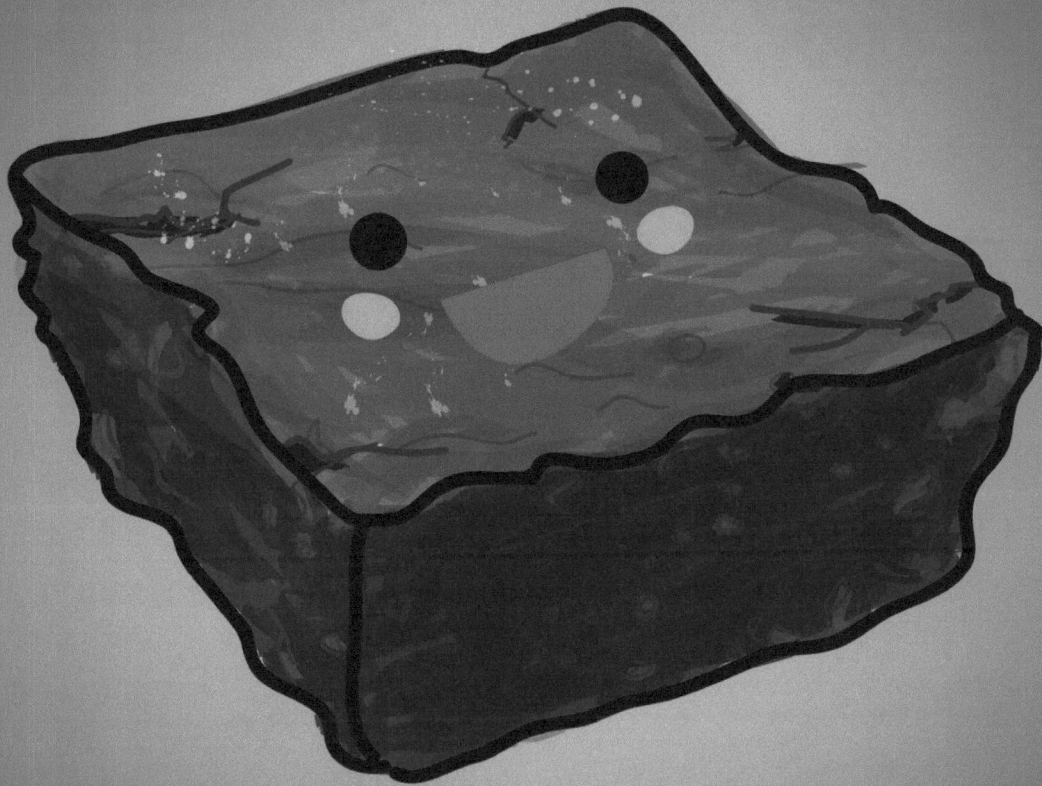

MACARONS

DANISH PASTRIES

DOUGHNUT

BISCUITS

GINGERBREAD

SWEET
ROLL